To all the teachers and coaches
who helped guide my own stubborn feet—J.B.

The path ahead will be both rugged and beautiful.
In difficult times try not to blame others.
Instead, remember young Jim Thorpe
and you will be given the gift of strength—S.D.N.

They say Jim Thorpe's story began in May of 1887 in a small log cabin on the North Canadian River. There in the Indian Territory that became the state of Oklahoma, Charlotte Vieux Thorpe, a Pottowatomie woman, gave birth to twin boys. Her husband, Hiram, a mixed-blood Indian of the Sac and Fox nation, stood close by on that spring day.

The sun was in Hiram Thorpe's heart as he looked down at the sons he named Charles and James. Jim's mother gave him another name.

"Wa-tho-huck," she said, thinking of how the light shone on the road to their cabin. "Bright Path."

As good as that name was, neither of them knew just how far that path would lead their son.

Like most twins, Jim and Charlie were close, even though they were not exactly the same. Charlie had darker skin and brown hair, while Jim's skin was light and his hair dark black. When they raced or wrestled, Jim was always a little ahead of Charlie, his best friend. Whenever Jim got too far ahead, he would stop and wait.

"Come on, Charlie," he would say with a grin.

Then, when his brother caught up, they would be off again.

Summer or winter, Jim and Charlie's favorite place was outdoors. They roamed the prairies, swam, and played together. By the time they were three, Pa Thorpe had taught his boys to ride a horse. He showed them how to shoot a bow, set a trap, and hunt. Jim took to it all like a catfish takes to a creek. Although small, he was quick and tough. He was so fast and had so much endurance that he could run down a rabbit on foot. When it came to the old ways, those skills that made the men of the Sac and Fox great providers for their families, Jim was a great learner. By the time the twins were six, Pa Thorpe said Jim knew more about the woods than many men.

Their sixth year also brought a big change for Jim and Charlie. The Indian Agency that oversaw the reservation said that when Sac and Fox children reached age six, they had to go to the Agency Boarding School. Indian boarding schools did not provide the same education offered to whites. Indian children were educated only to be maids or laborers. In addition the boarding schools were designed to cut them off from everything that made them Indians—their language, their traditions, even their families—and make them fit in with white society.

Jim's father had become one of the few Sac and Fox men who could read and write English. He'd seen uneducated Indians cheated out of everything by dishonest men who tricked the Indians into signing papers they could not read.

"My sons," he said to Jim and Charlie, "you need white man's knowledge to survive."

It was no surprise that Jim hated school. He had to wear awful clothes—a heavy wool suit, a felt cap, tight shoes, a shirt and necktie that strangled him. He also got smacked hard across his knuckles with a wooden ruler whenever he spoke a word of Sac. He missed Ma's cooking and Pa's stories about their clan ancestor, Chief Black Hawk, the famous warrior who had fought the whites to defend his people. Worst of all, school kept Jim inside all day and locked him up all night in a cold dormitory away from the forest and prairies. It made him feel like a fox caught in an iron trap. Jim didn't care about what school might do for him or his people. He just wanted to get away from it.

Charlie was better at his studies than Jim. He didn't seem to mind the military discipline or being stuck at a desk. Solving an arithmetic problem was a challenge to Charlie the way winning a race was to Jim. Now it was Charlie who was waiting for his brother to catch up.

"Come on, Jim," Charlie said. "Don't give up. You can do it."

So, Jim tried to master basic arithmetic, reading, and writing. Then, in his third year of school, something happened that broke his heart.

Sickness often struck the crowded, unheated dormitories of the Indian boarding schools. Sanitation was poor, and there were no real doctors to tend the sick. Epidemics of influenza swept through like prairie fires. Even common childhood diseases such as measles and whooping cough could be fatal to the Indian children jammed together in those schools.

Charlie was one of those who became sick. He caught pneumonia and died. Jim felt as if the sunlight had gone from his life. His twin brother had been his best friend.

Jim's mother tried to comfort her son, but he was inconsolable. He would never hear Charlie's encouraging voice again. The thought of going back to school without his brother tore at Jim's heart.

"Let me work around the farm, Pa," Jim begged.

His father, though, was sure he knew what was best.

"Son," he said, "you have to get an education. Charlie would have wanted you to keep learning."

Jim tried to listen to his father, but when he returned to school and saw the empty cot where Charlie had slept, it was too much for him. As soon as the teacher's back was turned, Jim ran the twenty-three miles back home, straight as an arrow.

Pa Thorpe had no choice but to send his stubborn son even farther away. So young Jim, at age eleven, was sent to Haskell Institute in Lawrence, Kansas, almost three hundred miles away.

Haskell was stricter than the Agency Boarding School. There children from more than eighty tribes were dressed in military uniforms and were awakened before dawn with a bugle call. Manual training was mixed with classroom studies to teach them trades useful to white society. Hard work was the rule, and the students of Haskell did it all—growing corn, making bread, building wagons, and sewing their own uniforms.

Jim did better at Haskell. He worked in the engineering shop. Learning how things were made was more interesting than being cooped up in a classroom.

Plus Haskell had something the Agency Boarding School didn't have—football. For the first time in his life, Jim saw a football game. The cheers of the crowd and the athleticism of the players wakened something deep inside Jim, the same emotions that had been stirred by Pa's stories of Black Hawk and the other warriors who had fought for their people. Jim knew right away that football was something he wanted to play.

But Jim was too small for the sport. He was less than five feet
tall and weighed just one hundred pounds. He joined the track
team instead and became one of the fastest runners. Meanwhile,
he watched every football game he could. Jim also met Chauncy
Archiquette, Haskell's best football player, who taught him about
the game. Chauncy even helped Jim make a little football out of
scrap leather stuffed with rags. With that football Jim organized
games with other boys too small for the school team.

Near the end of his second year at Haskell, Jim got word that his father had been shot in a hunting accident and was dying. Jim's only thought was that he had to get home. He ran off and headed south. It took him two weeks to reach their farm. To his surprise, Pa was there, recovered from his wound and waiting.

"We knew you were coming home," his father said, embracing him.

Jim never went back to Haskell. Shortly after he returned home, his mother died of a sudden illness. Jim grieved over the loss of his mother, and Pa Thorpe finally agreed that his son did not have to go back to boarding school.

Jim's father believed his son still needed education, so Jim began attending school nearby in Garden Grove. At Garden Grove, students were learning about a new thing called electricity. Electricity could make it seem as if the sun were still shining, even at night. The thought of that appealed to Jim. Electrical sunlight could be brought to Indian homes too. Pa Thorpe had always told Jim that education would give him the ability to help his people. Maybe becoming an electrician was the bright path he was supposed to follow.

One day a recruiter from the Carlisle Indian School in Pennsylvania came to Garden Grove. Carlisle was always looking for Indian students who were good athletes, and the recruiter had heard of Jim's success as a runner at Haskell.

"Would you like to be a Carlisle man?" the recruiter asked.

"Can I study electricity there?" Jim said.

"Of course," the recruiter replied, even though Carlisle offered no such course.

Something else also attracted Jim to Carlisle—sports. Carlisle was one of the first and most well-known of the Indian boarding schools. Everyone knew about the school and its amazing record of winning sports teams. The Carlisle Indians even beat teams from the big, famous colleges. At Carlisle, Jim thought, he could play football.

Pa Thorpe urged Jim to seize the opportunity. Somehow he knew Carlisle would be the first step on a trail that would lead his son to greatness.

"Son," he said, "you are an Indian. I want you to show other races what an Indian can do."

Soon after Jim arrived at Carlisle, he received bad news. His father had been bitten by a snake while working in his fields and had died of blood poisoning. The man who had fought so hard to force his son to get an education was gone.

Already a quiet person, Jim retreated further into silence after his father's death. But he did not desert Carlisle. Perhaps Jim felt the best way to remember his father was to live the dream Pa Thorpe had for him. It was now up to Jim to push himself.

The Carlisle system of sending new students off campus for work experience helped. Jim ended up at a farm in New Jersey. The farm labor reminded him of the many hours he had spent working by Pa's side in Oklahoma. Jim worked so hard and with such quiet confidence that everyone saw him as a man they could like and trust. To his delight, Jim was made foreman, head of all the workers.

When Jim came back to Carlisle in the fall, he was no longer a boy. He had grown taller, stronger, more self-assured. He was ready to play football, but he knew it would not be easy. Carlisle's famous coach Pop Warner would only allow the best to join his track squad or his football team as one of his "Athletic Boys."

One day Jim's big chance came. He was on his way to play a game of scrub football with some of his friends who were too small for the school team. As Jim crossed the field, he saw a group of varsity athletes practicing the high jump.

Jim asked if he could have a try, even though he was wearing overalls and an old pair of work shoes. The Athletic Boys snickered as they reset the bar for him. They placed it higher than anyone at Carlisle had ever jumped. Even in his work clothes, Jim cleared the bar on his first jump. No one could believe it. People stood around with their mouths wide open, staring. Jim just grinned and walked off to play football with his friends.

The next day Jim was told to report to the office of Coach Warner. Everyone knew Pop Warner was a great coach, but he was also a man with a bad temper. Jim wondered if Pop was going to yell at him for interrupting track practice.

"Do you know what you've done?" Pop Warner growled.

"Nothing bad, I hope," Jim said.

"Bad?" Pop Warner said. His face broke into a smile. "Boy, you've just broken the school record. Go down to the clubhouse and exchange those overalls for a track outfit. You're on my track team now."

Before long Jim Thorpe was Carlisle's best track athlete. He competed in the high jump, hurdles, and dashes, winning or placing in all of them. Still, Jim wanted to play football. Reluctantly Pop Warner told him he could give it a try.

Pop Warner didn't like the idea of his slender high jumper being injured in a football game, so he decided to discourage Jim by beginning his first practice with a tackling drill. Jim, the newcomer, had to take the ball and try to run from one end to the other, through the whole varsity team.

"Is that all?" Jim said. He looked at the football in his hands. It was the first time he'd ever held a real football, but he believed in himself. Then he took off down the field like a deer. He was past half the team before the players even saw him coming. At the other end Jim looked back. Behind him was the whole Carlisle team, the players holding nothing in their hands but air. There was a grin on Jim's face when he handed Coach Warner the ball.

"Doggone it," Pop Warner said. "You're supposed to give the first team tackling practice, not run through them." Pop Warner slammed the ball back into Jim's belly. "Do it again."

Jim's jaw was set as he ran the Carlisle gauntlet a second time. He was carrying not just a football, but the hopes and dreams of his family, his people, and all the Indians who had been told they could never compete with the white man. Tacklers bounced off Jim as he lowered his shoulders. No one stopped him. The sun shone around him as he stood in the end zone.

For years Jim had fought against his education. He had run away from it so many times. This time Jim used all he had learned from his mother's wisdom, his brother's encouragement, and his father's fierce determination that his son show what an Indian could do. From now on Jim Thorpe would run forward, toward the finish line, toward the goal. He didn't know how far he would go, but he believed in his journey. His education had put his feet on the bright path.

AUTHOR'S NOTE

That day, on the football field at Carlisle, a legend was born. The quiet American Indian boy from Oklahoma went on to international fame, and Jim Thorpe is now widely acknowledged as the dominant sports figure of the twentieth century.

At Carlisle Jim not only played football and ran track, he played lacrosse, was captain of the basketball team, and was the school's best tennis and handball player. His career there spanned six years, broken by a two-year stretch during which he played minor league baseball in North Carolina. That early foray into semiprofessional baseball, during which Jim pitched and played first base, would later come back to haunt him.

Jim Thorpe's two greatest college football years were 1911 and 1912. Starting on both offense and defense, he was also the team's kicker and leading tackler. On November 23, 1912, in the Springfield game, Jim scored all thirty of Carlisle's points, and at the end of the 1912

Running track for Carlisle

season, he was named an All American for the second year in a row. He continued to excel in track as well, setting collegiate records in thirteen different events. Although all Jim's records were eventually broken, no one had ever dominated as many events at one time. In fact, it seemed as if Jim could master any sport. He was an excellent golfer and bowler and a superior swimmer, billiards player, figure skater, gymnast, rower, and hockey player.

In 1912, coached by Pop Warner, Jim Thorpe went to the Summer Olympic Games in Stockholm, Sweden. There he won both the Pentathlon and the Decathlon. After placing the laurel wreath on Jim's head and handing him the gold medals, the king of Sweden extended his hand.

"Sir," King Gustav said, "you are the greatest athlete in the world."

Jim took his hand and shook it. "Thanks, King," he said.

Jim Thorpe had truly shown the world what an Indian could do. But sadly, in 1913 Jim's glory

Putting shot at Olympic Games

Playing football at Carlisle

at the Olympics was spoiled by the disclosure that he had played minor league baseball in 1909 and 1910. When asked if this was true, Jim freely admitted it. Many other college athletes did the same in those days, and Jim thought he had done nothing wrong. However, the Amateur Athletic Union ruled that as a professional, Jim should not have competed in the Olympics. He was stripped of his gold medals, and his name was removed from the Olympic record books.

Batting for New York Giants

Jim Thorpe went on to a great and varied career in professional sports. When he left college, he became a professional baseball player, and from 1913 to 1919 he played with the New York Giants, the Cincinnati Reds, and the Boston Braves. The big-time era of football began in 1915, when the professional game was reorganized. The Canton Bulldogs scored a publicity coup when they signed Jim Thorpe, by then the world's best-known American Indian as well as the world's most famous athlete. Jim led Canton to victory game after game, including three unofficial world championships. When the American Professional Football Association (later known as the National Football League) was formed in 1920, the members elected Jim Thorpe president. President or not, Jim kept playing until 1929 for teams including the New York Giants and the Oorang Indians. By age forty-two, even Jim was too old for pro football, and he retired.

Jim Thorpe was a determined but gentle person with a great sense of humor and an unforgettable grin, a modest man whose greatest virtue was his love of honesty. He gave inspiring lectures around the country about his career and the importance of providing equal rights and opportunities for American Indians. "I would like to ask every one of you here to work for the improvement of Indian conditions," Jim would often say at the end of his talks. His eloquent words affected the lives of countless people, who held him up as a fine example of what an Indian could do.

Married three times, Jim Thorpe had five sons and three daughters. After his death in 1953, his children tried to follow his example of fighting for Indian rights. His daughter Grace, an activist with the National Congress of American Indians, also devoted herself to ensuring that her father's athletic accomplishments would not be forgotten. Through her efforts and those of many others, the Amateur Athletic Union restored Jim's status as an amateur, and the International Olympic Committee reversed its decision in 1982. In 1983 duplicate gold medals were given to the Thorpe family. Jim Thorpe's path was bright again.

Displaying sprint start form for young athletes

IMPORTANT DATES IN JIM THORPE'S LIFE AND LEGACY

1887* James Francis Thorpe and twin brother, Charles, born on Sac and Fox Indian Reservation along North Canadian River in Oklahoma May 28

Jim, left, and Charlie, age 3

1893 Enters Agency Boarding School with Charlie

1896 Charlie dies of pneumonia

1898 Arrives at Haskell Institute in Lawrence, Kansas

1902* Charlotte Thorpe (mother) dies; begins attending school in Garden Grove, Oklahoma

1904 Enters United States Indian Industrial School in Carlisle, Pennsylvania; Hiram Thorpe (father) dies

Carlisle campus

1907–1912 Plays college football

1909–1910 Plays minor league baseball

1911, 1912 Named First Team All American Halfback at Carlisle

1912 Wins gold medals in Pentathlon and Decathlon at Summer Olympic Games in Stockholm, Sweden

Original Olympic gold medals

1913 Stripped of Olympic gold medals and name removed from record books

1913–1919 Plays major league baseball

1915–1929 Plays professional football

1917 Becomes a United States citizen

1920 Elected first president of American Professional Football Association (now National Football League)

1922 Forms Oorang Indians, an all-Indian professional football team

1929 Retires from professional football at age forty-two

1950 Voted America's Greatest Football Player and Greatest All-Around Male Athlete of first half century by Associated Press

1951 World premiere of movie *Jim Thorpe, All American,* starring Burt Lancaster as Thorpe

1953 Dies March 28; buried in Mauch Chunk, Pennsylvania, which later is renamed Jim Thorpe, Pennsylvania

1958 Elected to National Indian Hall of Fame

1963 Inducted into Pro Football Hall of Fame as part of original class

Thorpe statue in Pro Football Hall of Fame

1973 Amateur Athletic Union reverses 1913 decision and changes Thorpe's status to amateur

1975 Inducted into National Track & Field Hall of Fame

1982 International Olympic Committee restores Thorpe's name to record books

1983 Duplicate Olympic gold medals given to Thorpe family; inducted into U.S. Olympic Hall of Fame

1998 U.S. Postal Service issues Jim Thorpe commemorative stamp as part of its Celebrate the Century program

1999 Resolution put forth in U.S. Congress to recognize Thorpe as America's Athlete of the Century

2000 Voted Athlete of the Century by ABC's *Wide World of Sports*

2001 Memorialized on Wheaties® The Breakfast of Champions cereal box

*Date cited obtained from Thorpe family or most reliable sources

JIM THORPE'S
B _____ H

ILl 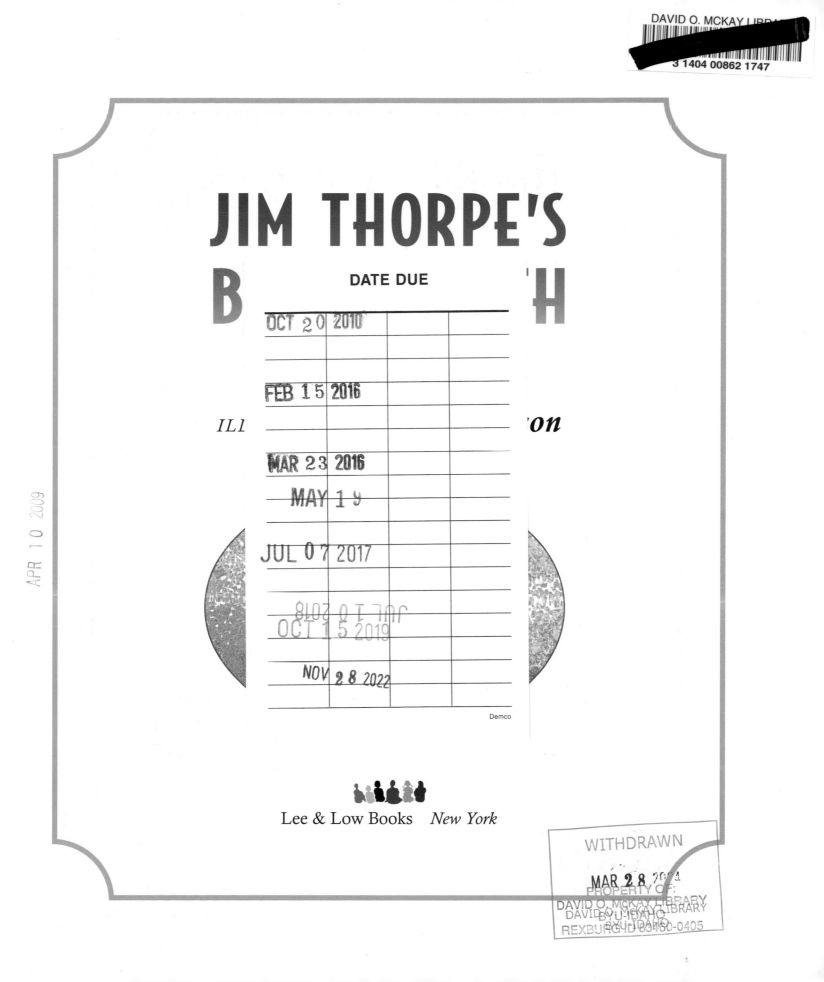 _on_

Lee & Low Books   _New York_

LEE & LOW BOOKS Inc., 95 Madison Avenue, New York, NY 10016
leeandlow.com

Acknowledgments
My inspiration to write a book for young readers about Jim Thorpe came from two people and two songs. The first was Swift Eagle, an Apache/Pueblo elder who worked with Jim in Hollywood. Swifty started me thinking about this project more than twenty years ago when he taught me a song Jim Thorpe had given him in 1935. The second was my good friend and fellow former athlete Jack Gladstone, a Blackfeet folk singer. Jack's wonderful song about Jim, "Bright Path," was and remains an inspiration to me.

It is also important to recognize that many people worked very hard over the years to pass on Jim Thorpe's legacy and restore the Olympic medals that were taken from him. None deserve more credit than his children, especially his daughter Grace Thorpe. Like her father, she has been a strong voice for Native American rights. I deeply appreciate the help she gave me.

Of all the books written about Jim Thorpe, the best picture of this unique American Indian hero's life is found in Robert L. Whitman's *Jim Thorpe, Athlete of the Century: A Pictorial Biography.* I express my sincere gratitude to Bob for his advice and critical input.

Thanks, too, to Barbara Landis of the Carlisle Historical Society for her suggestions and for sharing back issues of the Carlisle Indian School newsletter, *The Indian Helper.* There are still so many true stories that need to be told about the victories won by Indian children who tried their best, against unimaginable odds, at schools such as Carlisle. I just hope this book is worthy of them and their families, of Jim Thorpe and his family, and of all those—past, present, and future—touched by his great life. —J. B.

Manufactured in China

Book design by Christy Hale
Book production by The Kids at Our House

The text is set in Calisto
The illustrations are rendered in acrylic

(HC) 10 9 8 7 6 5 4
(PB) 10 9 8 7 6 5 4 3 2 1
First Edition

Library of Congress Cataloging-in-Publication Data
Bruchac, Joseph.
Jim Thorpe's bright path / by Joseph Bruchac ; illustrated by S. D. Nelson.— 1st ed.
p. cm.
Summary: A biography of Native American athlete Jim Thorpe, focusing on how his boyhood education set the stage for his athletic achievements which gained him international fame and Olympic gold medals. Author's note details Thorpe's life after college.
ISBN 978-1-58430-166-0 (hardcover)
ISBN 978-1-60060-340-2 (paperback)
1. Thorpe, Jim, 1887-1953—Juvenile literature. 2. Athletes—United States—Biography—Juvenile literature. 3. Indian athletes—United States—Biography—Juvenile literature. [1. Thorpe, Jim 1887-1953. 2. Athletes. 3. Indians of North America—Biography.] I. Nelson, S.D., ill. II. Title.
GV697.T5B78 2004
796'.092—dc21   2003008993